THE COOK'S BOOK

A Promised Land Production

THE COOK'S BOOK
Recipes from My Kitchen

Illustrations by Claudia Karabaic Sargent

Grove Weidenfeld
New York

For Bru, who loved good food almost as much as he loved his friends.

—C.K.S.

Published by Grove Weidenfeld, New York
A Division of Wheatland Corporation
841 Broadway
New York, New York 10003-4793

Published in Canada by General Publishing Company, Ltd.

International Standard Book Number 1-55584-398-0

Type design by Jack Eckstein

Manufactured in the United States of America

First Edition

10 9 8 7 6 5 4 3 2 1

This book was given to

_____

by

_____

on

_____

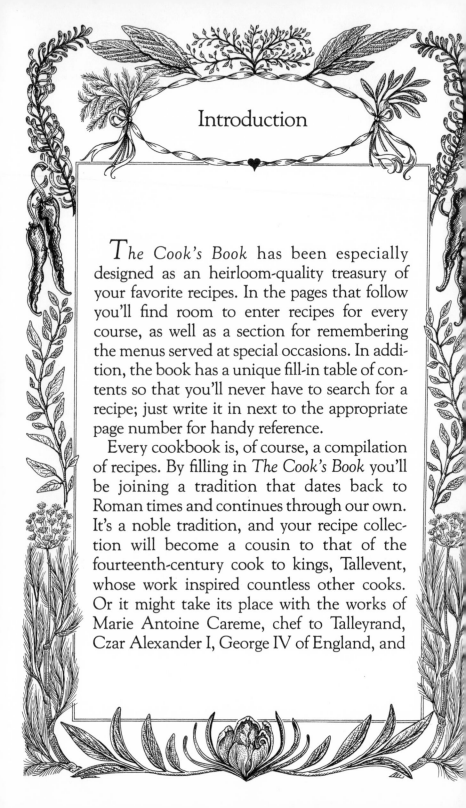

Introduction

The Cook's Book has been especially designed as an heirloom-quality treasury of your favorite recipes. In the pages that follow you'll find room to enter recipes for every course, as well as a section for remembering the menus served at special occasions. In addition, the book has a unique fill-in table of contents so that you'll never have to search for a recipe; just write it in next to the appropriate page number for handy reference.

Every cookbook is, of course, a compilation of recipes. By filling in *The Cook's Book* you'll be joining a tradition that dates back to Roman times and continues through our own. It's a noble tradition, and your recipe collection will become a cousin to that of the fourteenth-century cook to kings, Tallevent, whose work inspired countless other cooks. Or it might take its place with the works of Marie Antoine Careme, chef to Talleyrand, Czar Alexander I, George IV of England, and

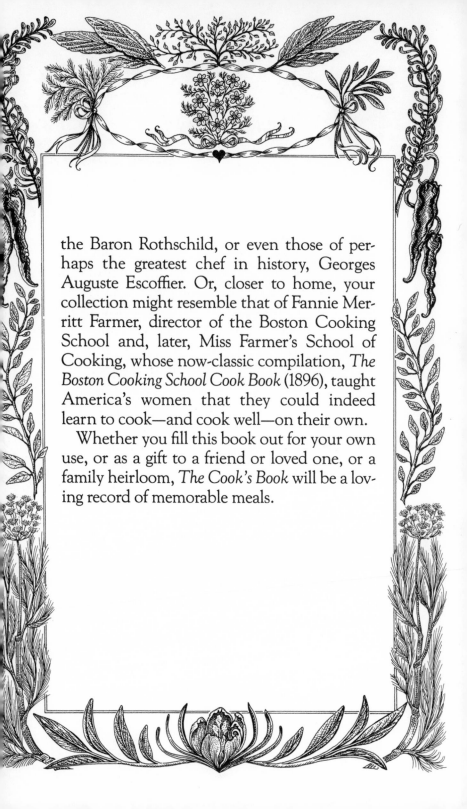

the Baron Rothschild, or even those of perhaps the greatest chef in history, Georges Auguste Escoffier. Or, closer to home, your collection might resemble that of Fannie Merritt Farmer, director of the Boston Cooking School and, later, Miss Farmer's School of Cooking, whose now-classic compilation, *The Boston Cooking School Cook Book* (1896), taught America's women that they could indeed learn to cook—and cook well—on their own.

Whether you fill this book out for your own use, or as a gift to a friend or loved one, or a family heirloom, *The Cook's Book* will be a loving record of memorable meals.

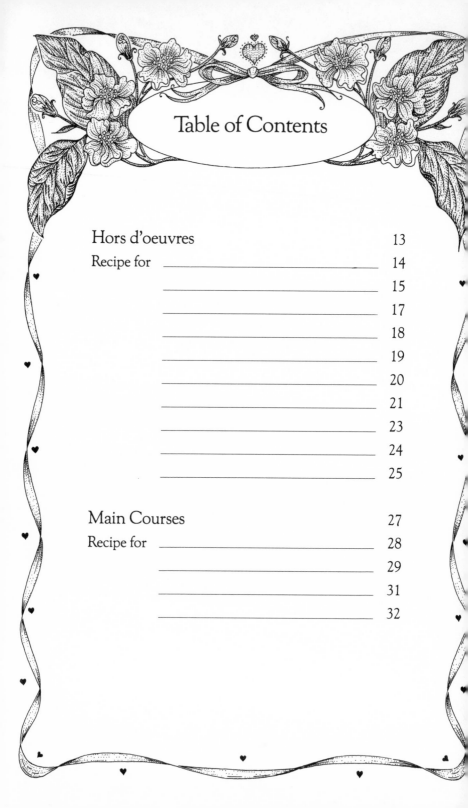

Table of Contents

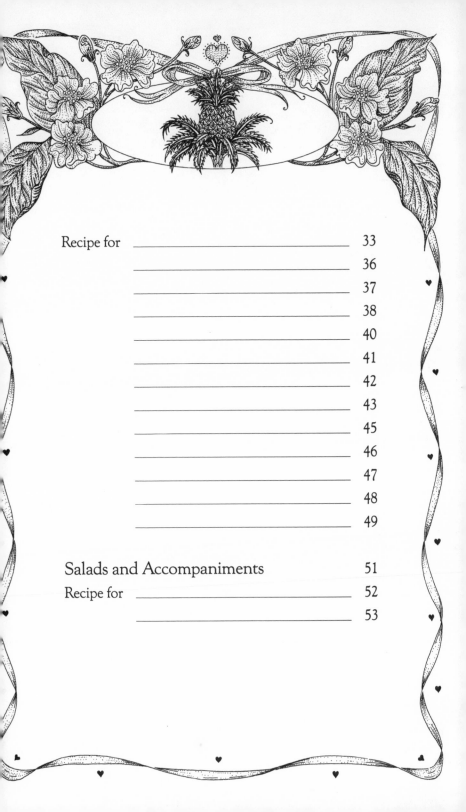

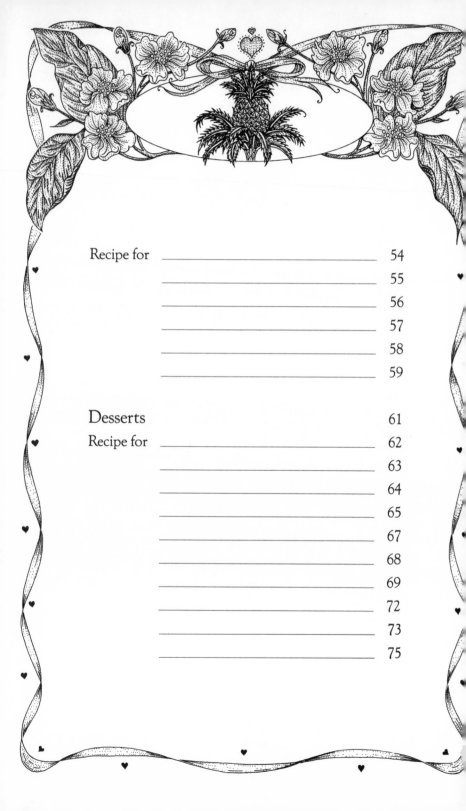

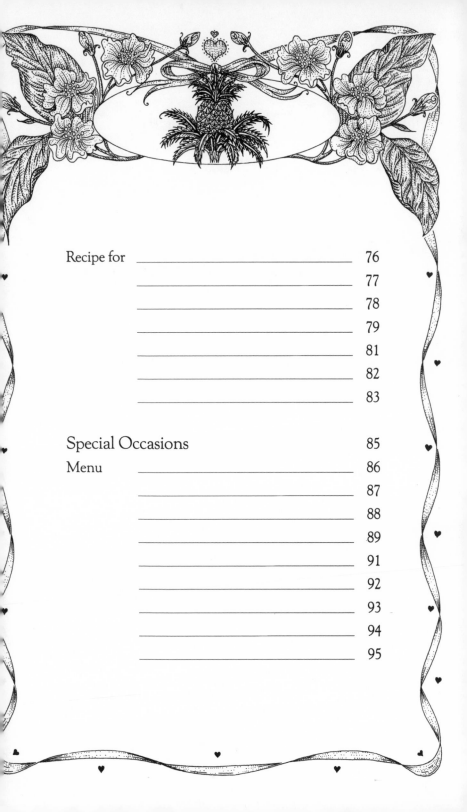

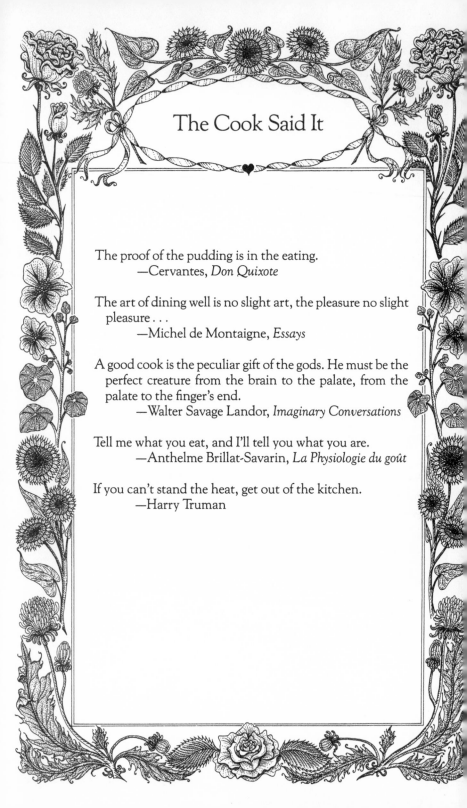

The Cook Said It

The proof of the pudding is in the eating.
  —Cervantes, *Don Quixote*

The art of dining well is no slight art, the pleasure no slight
  pleasure . . .
  —Michel de Montaigne, *Essays*

A good cook is the peculiar gift of the gods. He must be the
  perfect creature from the brain to the palate, from the
  palate to the finger's end.
  —Walter Savage Landor, *Imaginary Conversations*

Tell me what you eat, and I'll tell you what you are.
  —Anthelme Brillat-Savarin, *La Physiologie du goût*

If you can't stand the heat, get out of the kitchen.
  —Harry Truman

Hors d'oeuvres

Recipe name

Ingredients

Oven Temperature

Cooking Time

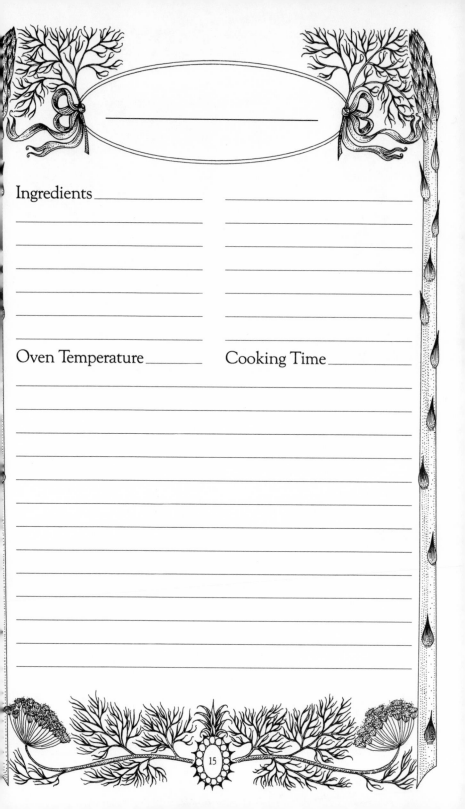

Ingredients

Oven Temperature _____ Cooking Time _____

Ingredients

Oven Temperature_____   Cooking Time_____

Ingredients

Oven Temperature

Cooking Time

Ingredients _____

_____

_____

_____

_____

_____

_____

Oven Temperature_____   Cooking Time_____

_____

Ingredients _____   _____

_____   _____

_____   _____

_____   _____

_____   _____

_____   _____

_____

Oven Temperature_____   Cooking Time_____

_____

_____

_____

_____

_____

_____

_____

_____

_____

_____

_____

_____

_____

_____

Ingredients_____   _____

_____   _____

_____   _____

_____   _____

_____   _____

_____   _____

Oven Temperature_____   Cooking Time_____

_____

_____

_____

_____

_____

_____

_____

_____

_____

_____

_____

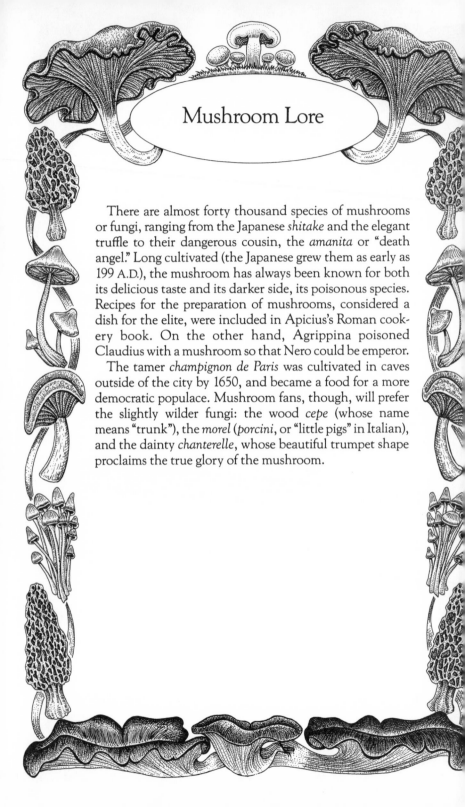

Mushroom Lore

There are almost forty thousand species of mushrooms or fungi, ranging from the Japanese *shitake* and the elegant truffle to their dangerous cousin, the *amanita* or "death angel." Long cultivated (the Japanese grew them as early as 199 A.D.), the mushroom has always been known for both its delicious taste and its darker side, its poisonous species. Recipes for the preparation of mushrooms, considered a dish for the elite, were included in Apicius's Roman cookery book. On the other hand, Agrippina poisoned Claudius with a mushroom so that Nero could be emperor.

The tamer *champignon de Paris* was cultivated in caves outside of the city by 1650, and became a food for a more democratic populace. Mushroom fans, though, will prefer the slightly wilder fungi: the wood *cepe* (whose name means "trunk"), the *morel* (*porcini*, or "little pigs" in Italian), and the dainty *chanterelle*, whose beautiful trumpet shape proclaims the true glory of the mushroom.

Ingredients

Oven Temperature

Cooking Time

Ingredients

Oven Temperature_____   Cooking Time_____

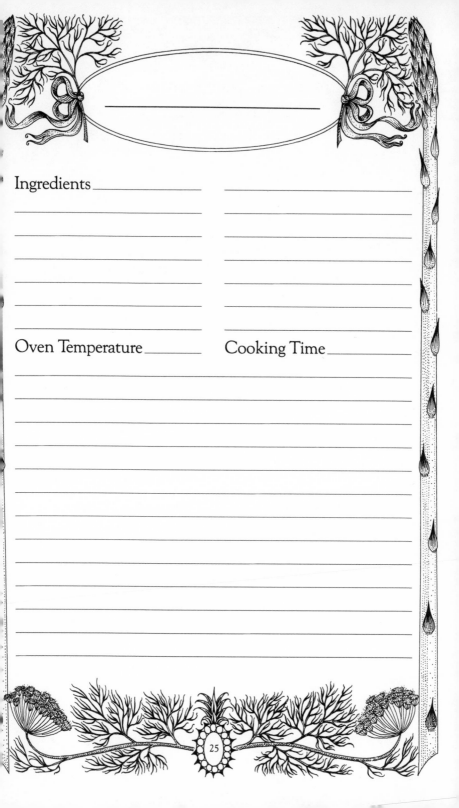

Ingredients

Oven Temperature_____ Cooking Time_____

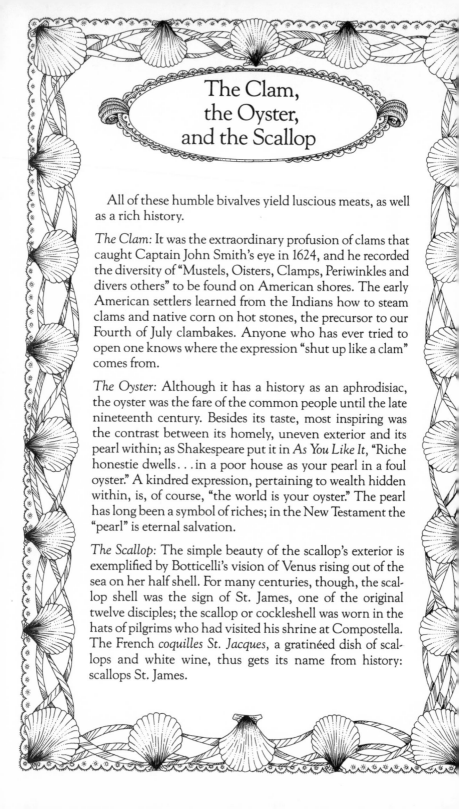

The Clam,
the Oyster,
and the Scallop

All of these humble bivalves yield luscious meats, as well as a rich history.

The Clam: It was the extraordinary profusion of clams that caught Captain John Smith's eye in 1624, and he recorded the diversity of "Mustels, Oisters, Clamps, Periwinkles and divers others" to be found on American shores. The early American settlers learned from the Indians how to steam clams and native corn on hot stones, the precursor to our Fourth of July clambakes. Anyone who has ever tried to open one knows where the expression "shut up like a clam" comes from.

The Oyster: Although it has a history as an aphrodisiac, the oyster was the fare of the common people until the late nineteenth century. Besides its taste, most inspiring was the contrast between its homely, uneven exterior and its pearl within; as Shakespeare put it in *As You Like It*, "Riche honestie dwells. . .in a poor house as your pearl in a foul oyster." A kindred expression, pertaining to wealth hidden within, is, of course, "the world is your oyster." The pearl has long been a symbol of riches; in the New Testament the "pearl" is eternal salvation.

The Scallop: The simple beauty of the scallop's exterior is exemplified by Botticelli's vision of Venus rising out of the sea on her half shell. For many centuries, though, the scallop shell was the sign of St. James, one of the original twelve disciples; the scallop or cockleshell was worn in the hats of pilgrims who had visited his shrine at Compostella. The French *coquilles St. Jacques*, a gratinéed dish of scallops and white wine, thus gets its name from history: scallops St. James.

Main Courses

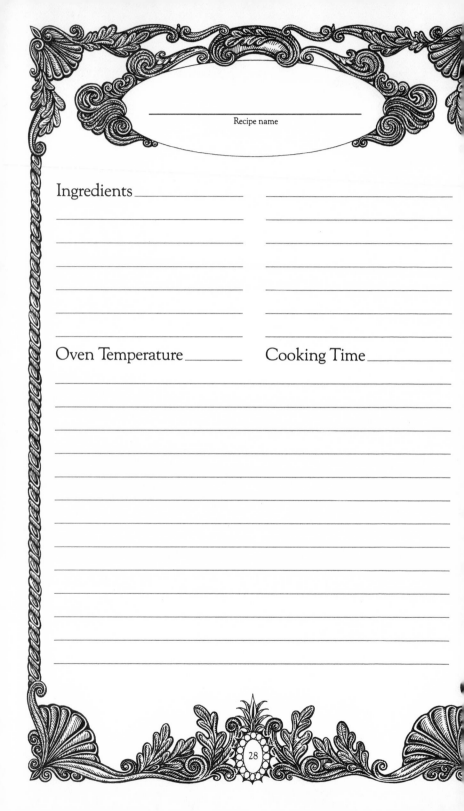

_____
Recipe name

Ingredients_____ _____

_____ _____

_____ _____

_____ _____

_____ _____

_____ _____

Oven Temperature_____ Cooking Time_____

_____

_____

_____

_____

_____

_____

_____

_____

_____

_____

_____

_____

_____

_____

Ingredients_____

_____

Oven Temperature_____ Cooking Time_____

Ingredients

Oven Temperature_____   Cooking Time_____

Ingredients

Oven Temperature_____   Cooking Time_____

Ingredients _____   _____
_____   _____
_____   _____
_____   _____
_____   _____
_____   _____
_____   _____

Oven Temperature_____   Cooking Time_____

_____
_____
_____
_____
_____
_____
_____
_____
_____
_____
_____
_____
_____
_____

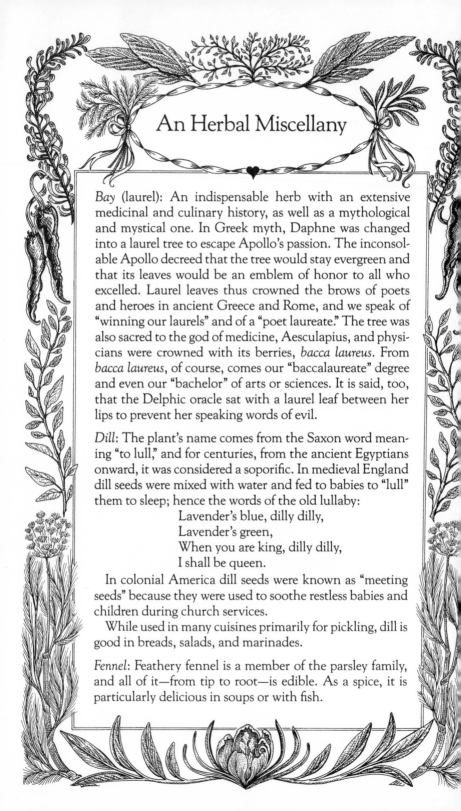

An Herbal Miscellany

Bay (laurel): An indispensable herb with an extensive medicinal and culinary history, as well as a mythological and mystical one. In Greek myth, Daphne was changed into a laurel tree to escape Apollo's passion. The inconsolable Apollo decreed that the tree would stay evergreen and that its leaves would be an emblem of honor to all who excelled. Laurel leaves thus crowned the brows of poets and heroes in ancient Greece and Rome, and we speak of "winning our laurels" and of a "poet laureate." The tree was also sacred to the god of medicine, Aesculapius, and physicians were crowned with its berries, *bacca laureus*. From *bacca laureus*, of course, comes our "baccalaureate" degree and even our "bachelor" of arts or sciences. It is said, too, that the Delphic oracle sat with a laurel leaf between her lips to prevent her speaking words of evil.

Dill: The plant's name comes from the Saxon word meaning "to lull," and for centuries, from the ancient Egyptians onward, it was considered a soporific. In medieval England dill seeds were mixed with water and fed to babies to "lull" them to sleep; hence the words of the old lullaby:

> Lavender's blue, dilly dilly,
> Lavender's green,
> When you are king, dilly dilly,
> I shall be queen.

In colonial America dill seeds were known as "meeting seeds" because they were used to soothe restless babies and children during church services.

While used in many cuisines primarily for pickling, dill is good in breads, salads, and marinades.

Fennel: Feathery fennel is a member of the parsley family, and all of it—from tip to root—is edible. As a spice, it is particularly delicious in soups or with fish.

For the ancient Greeks and Romans fennel symbolized victory in battle, and soldiers ate it for fortitude; in the eighteenth century it was gathered in a "Sabbath day posy," carried to church and believed to be an aid against the devil. (It was also thought to help spiritual salvation since it was said to rouse weary churchgoers who might otherwise doze off during services.) As a remedy, fennel has been thought to cure everything from failing eyesight to obesity; it was also used as an aphrodisiac.

Marjoram: The Greek name of this pretty plant, *originum*, means "mountain joy." Traditionally it was used medicinally to cure depression, but for the modern cook it is more likely to lift the taste of pork and veal, soups and stews, than the spirit of the chef.

Parsley: The ancient Greeks dedicated this herb to Persephone, goddess of the underworld, and wreaths of it adorned the ancient tombs. Sacred to the dead and to the heroic (Homer relates that warriors fed it to the chariot horses), it was not used for cooking until the fifteenth century.

Saffron: One of the most precious of herbs, in part for the difficulty of its harvest, saffron is the dried stigma of the golden crocus. A single flower has only three stigmas, each of which must be picked by hand! It is said that one hundred thousand flowers are needed to yield a pound of saffron.

The principal source of yellow dye in the ancient world, saffron has also long been used as a condiment and perfume. The Persians revered the flower as a symbol of the sun, and the spice itself is mentioned in sources as diverse as Homer and the Song of Solomon.

Ingredients _____

_____
_____
_____
_____
_____
_____

Oven Temperature_____   Cooking Time_____

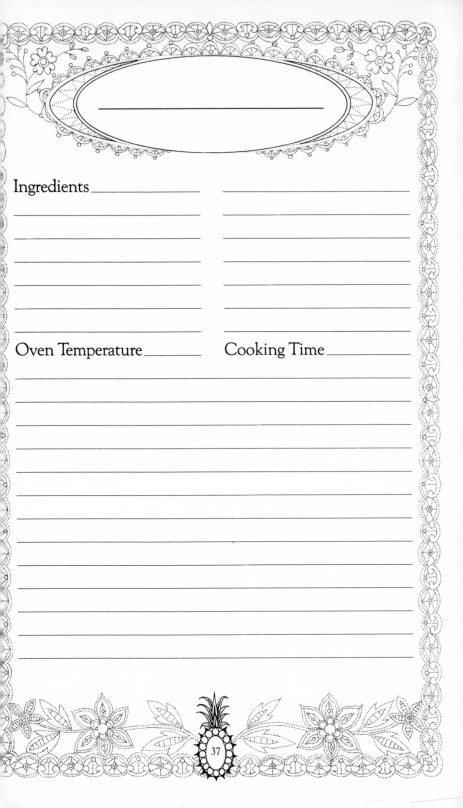

Ingredients _____ _____
_____ _____
_____ _____
_____ _____
_____ _____
_____ _____

Oven Temperature _____ **Cooking Time** _____

_____
_____
_____
_____
_____
_____
_____
_____
_____
_____
_____
_____
_____

Ingredients

Oven Temperature _____   Cooking Time _____

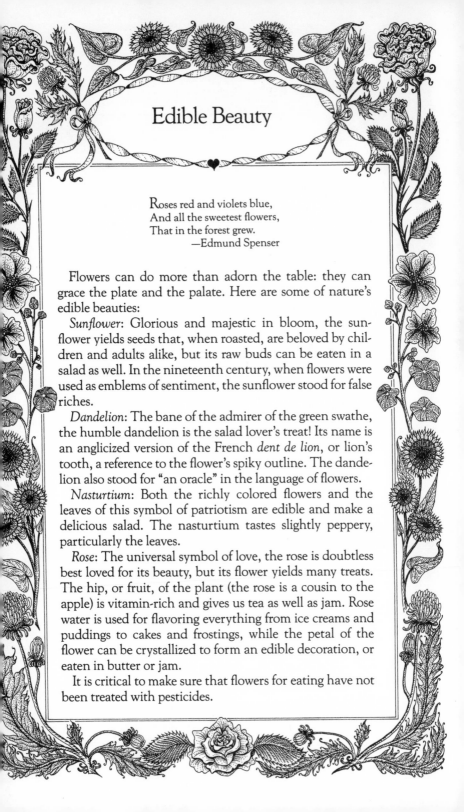

Edible Beauty

Roses red and violets blue,
And all the sweetest flowers,
That in the forest grew.
—Edmund Spenser

Flowers can do more than adorn the table: they can grace the plate and the palate. Here are some of nature's edible beauties:

Sunflower: Glorious and majestic in bloom, the sunflower yields seeds that, when roasted, are beloved by children and adults alike, but its raw buds can be eaten in a salad as well. In the nineteenth century, when flowers were used as emblems of sentiment, the sunflower stood for false riches.

Dandelion: The bane of the admirer of the green swathe, the humble dandelion is the salad lover's treat! Its name is an anglicized version of the French *dent de lion*, or lion's tooth, a reference to the flower's spiky outline. The dandelion also stood for "an oracle" in the language of flowers.

Nasturtium: Both the richly colored flowers and the leaves of this symbol of patriotism are edible and make a delicious salad. The nasturtium tastes slightly peppery, particularly the leaves.

Rose: The universal symbol of love, the rose is doubtless best loved for its beauty, but its flower yields many treats. The hip, or fruit, of the plant (the rose is a cousin to the apple) is vitamin-rich and gives us tea as well as jam. Rose water is used for flavoring everything from ice creams and puddings to cakes and frostings, while the petal of the flower can be crystallized to form an edible decoration, or eaten in butter or jam.

It is critical to make sure that flowers for eating have not been treated with pesticides.

Ingredients _____   _____
_____   _____
_____   _____
_____   _____
_____   _____
_____   _____
_____   _____

Oven Temperature _____   Cooking Time _____

_____
_____
_____
_____
_____
_____
_____
_____
_____
_____
_____
_____
_____
_____
_____

Ingredients

Oven Temperature

Cooking Time

Ingredients _____

Oven Temperature _____   Cooking Time _____

_____

Ingredients _____   _____

_____   _____

_____   _____

_____   _____

_____   _____

_____   _____

Oven Temperature_____   Cooking Time_____

The Culinary Bard

During Shakespeare's time the main meal—a copious and sometimes opulent one—was served at midday. Elizabeth I's reign was a time of prosperity, and the role of food in Shakespeare's plays makes it clear he knew what his audience liked.

Lest we forget, it's at a sumptuous banquet that the ghost of Banquo appears in *Macbeth*, and Romeo and Juliet meet at a dance preceded by a feast. Shakespeare knew about leftovers too: as the servants plan their own party from what's left, one of them, still hard at work, begs the other to save him a piece of "marchpane," a sweetmeat with almonds. (I, iv) The attention is on food as well when the Capulets, ignorant of Juliet's secret vows to Romeo, prepare for her wedding to Paris: the nurse fetches spices, dates, and quinces, while old Capulet cries out, "Look to the baked meats, sweet Angelica sold us/Spare not the cost." (IV, iv)

Cleopatra refers to the "salad days" of her youth as past, while the means of her suicide—an asp—is hidden in a basket of figs. And King Lear is first shown to be no longer the master of his house when his cries for "Dinner, ho, dinner!" are ignored by the servants.

And who can forget Falstaff's famous tavern bill in *Henry IV*, Part I:

> Item, A capon . . . . 2s. 2d.
> Item, sauce . . . . 4d.
> Item, Sack two gallons . . . . 5s. 8d.
> Item, bread . . . . ob.

It's the preponderance of "sack," or Spanish wine, that elicits the prince's attention: "O monstrous! but one half-penny worth of bread to this intolerable deal of sack!"

Food for thought indeed.

Ingredients _____ _____
_____ _____
_____ _____
_____ _____
_____ _____
_____ _____
_____ _____

Oven Temperature _____ Cooking Time _____
_____
_____
_____
_____
_____
_____
_____
_____
_____
_____
_____
_____

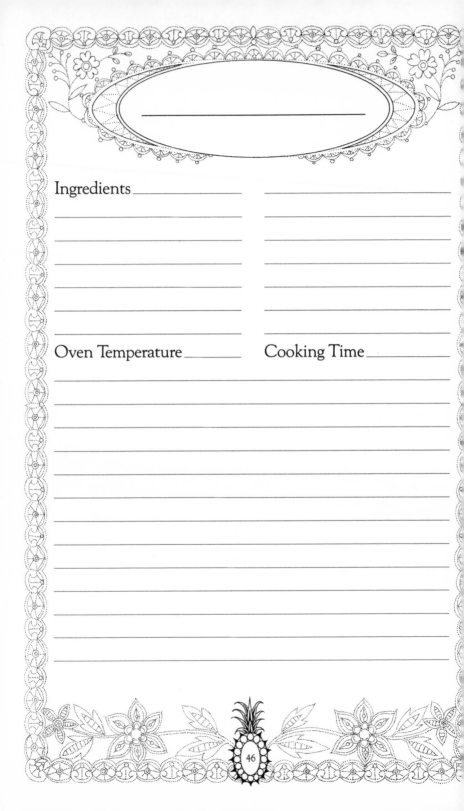

Ingredients

Oven Temperature

Cooking Time

Ingredients _____

Oven Temperature _____ Cooking Time _____

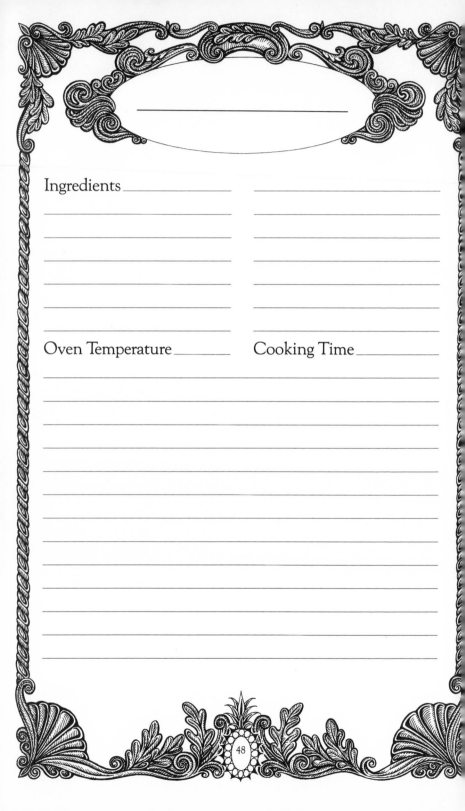

Ingredients _____   _____

_____   _____

_____   _____

_____   _____

_____   _____

_____   _____

Oven Temperature_____   Cooking Time_____

_____

_____

_____

_____

_____

_____

_____

_____

_____

_____

_____

_____

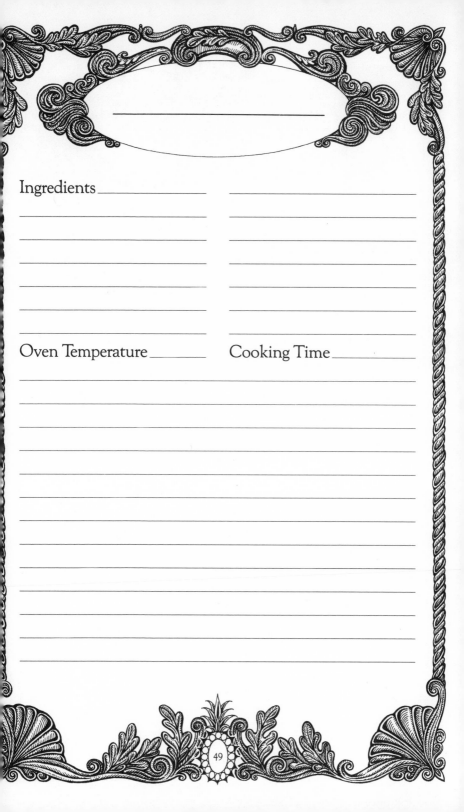

Ingredients_____ _____

_____ _____

_____ _____

_____ _____

_____ _____

_____ _____

Oven Temperature_____ Cooking Time_____

_____

_____

_____

_____

_____

_____

_____

_____

_____

_____

_____

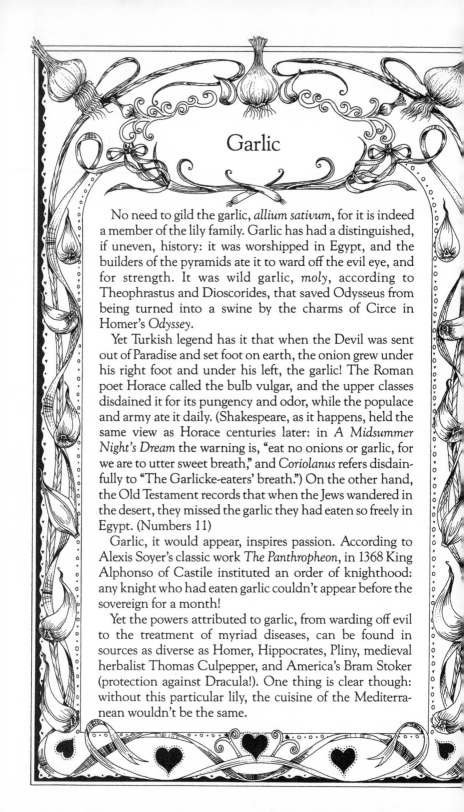

Garlic

No need to gild the garlic, *allium sativum,* for it is indeed a member of the lily family. Garlic has had a distinguished, if uneven, history: it was worshipped in Egypt, and the builders of the pyramids ate it to ward off the evil eye, and for strength. It was wild garlic, *moly,* according to Theophrastus and Dioscorides, that saved Odysseus from being turned into a swine by the charms of Circe in Homer's *Odyssey.*

Yet Turkish legend has it that when the Devil was sent out of Paradise and set foot on earth, the onion grew under his right foot and under his left, the garlic! The Roman poet Horace called the bulb vulgar, and the upper classes disdained it for its pungency and odor, while the populace and army ate it daily. (Shakespeare, as it happens, held the same view as Horace centuries later: in *A Midsummer Night's Dream* the warning is, "eat no onions or garlic, for we are to utter sweet breath," and *Coriolanus* refers disdainfully to "The Garlicke-eaters' breath.") On the other hand, the Old Testament records that when the Jews wandered in the desert, they missed the garlic they had eaten so freely in Egypt. (Numbers 11)

Garlic, it would appear, inspires passion. According to Alexis Soyer's classic work *The Panthropheon,* in 1368 King Alphonso of Castile instituted an order of knighthood: any knight who had eaten garlic couldn't appear before the sovereign for a month!

Yet the powers attributed to garlic, from warding off evil to the treatment of myriad diseases, can be found in sources as diverse as Homer, Hippocrates, Pliny, medieval herbalist Thomas Culpepper, and America's Bram Stoker (protection against Dracula!). One thing is clear though: without this particular lily, the cuisine of the Mediterranean wouldn't be the same.

Salads and Accompaniments

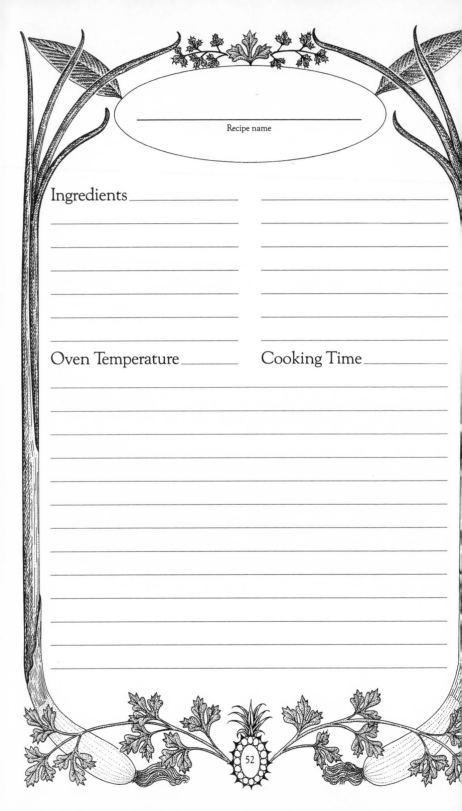

_____
Recipe name

Ingredients _____   _____

_____   _____

_____   _____

_____   _____

_____   _____

_____   _____

Oven Temperature_____   Cooking Time_____

_____

_____

_____

_____

_____

_____

_____

_____

_____

_____

_____

_____

Ingredients _____

_____

_____

_____

_____

_____

_____

Oven Temperature _____   Cooking Time _____

_____

_____

_____

_____

_____

_____

_____

_____

_____

_____

_____

Ingredients_____   _____

_____   _____
_____   _____
_____   _____
_____   _____
_____   _____
_____

Oven Temperature_____   Cooking Time_____

_____
_____
_____
_____
_____
_____
_____
_____
_____
_____
_____
_____

Ingredients _____

Oven Temperature_____

Cooking Time_____

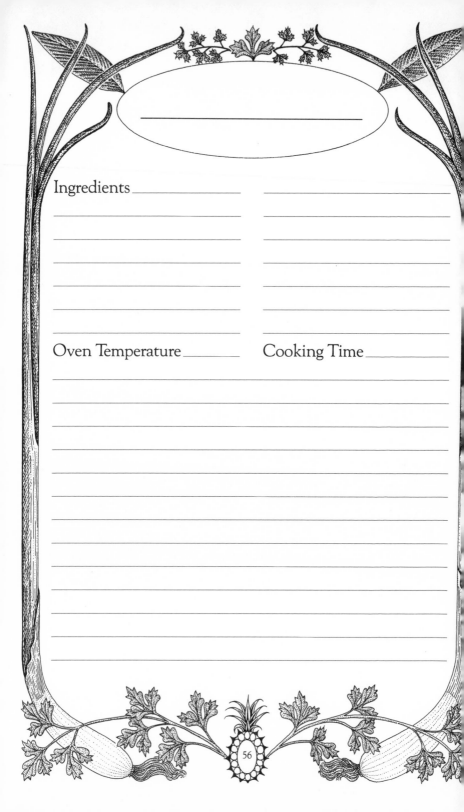

Ingredients

Oven Temperature_____ Cooking Time_____

Ingredients_____ _____
_____ _____
_____ _____
_____ _____
_____ _____
_____ _____
_____

Oven Temperature_____ Cooking Time_____
_____
_____
_____
_____
_____
_____
_____
_____
_____
_____
_____
_____
_____

Ingredients _____ _____

Oven Temperature _____ Cooking Time _____

Ingredients_____ _____

Oven Temperature_____ Cooking Time_____

Inventions

Necessity is sometimes, but not always, the mother of invention. Some of the following are felicitous accidents, some, planned steps in culinary invention:

The tea bag: An accidental find if there ever was one. Thomas Sullivan, a New York tea importer, sent out his tea samples in silk bags, rather than tins, just to save some money. His customers ordered the bags, finding them a handy way of brewing.

Margarine: When in 1869 cattle were devastated by a plague and butter was scarce, France's Napoleon II offered a prize for the invention of something to take the place of butter. A French chemist invented it but never got to produce it since France went to war with Prussia. He did, however, sell his patent to the enterprising Dutch, who produced the first margarine.

The ice cream cone: It was blisteringly hot at the 1904 St. Louis World's Fair and, according to food historian Margaret Visser, an immigrant, Ernest Hamir, had the bright idea of rolling up a Persian waffle and placing the ice cream atop it. It should be noted, though, that others have claimed to have invented the cone as well. As it happens, that hot World's Fair was the spawning ground for another culinary first: iced tea. One Richard Blechynden, promoting the teas of India and Ceylon, could find no taker for his fare in the heat—until he got the bright idea of dumping some ice cubes in the brew. *Voila!*

Desserts

_____
Recipe name

Ingredients_____   _____

_____   _____

_____   _____

_____   _____

_____   _____

_____   _____

Oven Temperature_____   Cooking Time_____

_____

_____

_____

_____

_____

_____

_____

_____

_____

_____

_____

Ingredients _____   _____
_____   _____
_____   _____
_____   _____
_____   _____
_____   _____

Oven Temperature _____   Cooking Time _____

_____
_____
_____
_____
_____
_____
_____
_____
_____
_____
_____
_____
_____

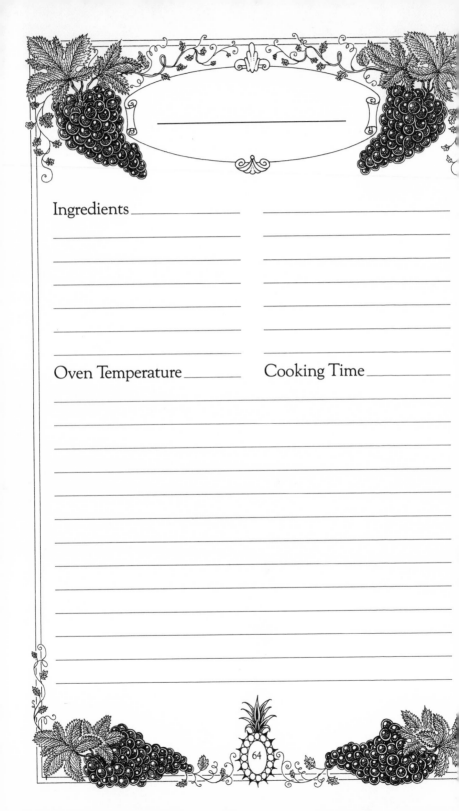

Ingredients _____ _____

_____ _____

_____ _____

_____ _____

_____ _____

_____ _____

Oven Temperature _____ Cooking Time _____

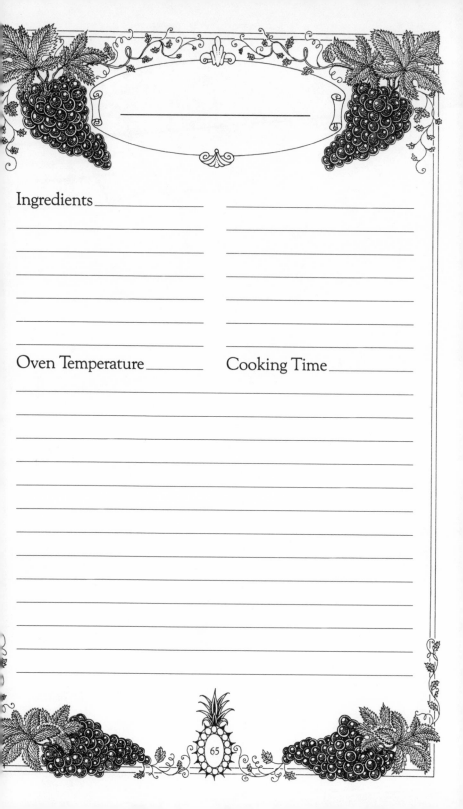

Ingredients

Oven Temperature

Cooking Time

Ingredients _____ _____

Oven Temperature_____ Cooking Time_____

Ingredients_____   _____

_____   _____

_____   _____

_____   _____

_____   _____

_____   _____

Oven Temperature_____   Cooking Time_____

_____

_____

_____

_____

_____

_____

_____

_____

_____

_____

_____

_____

Ingredients _____ _____

Oven Temperature _____ Cooking Time _____

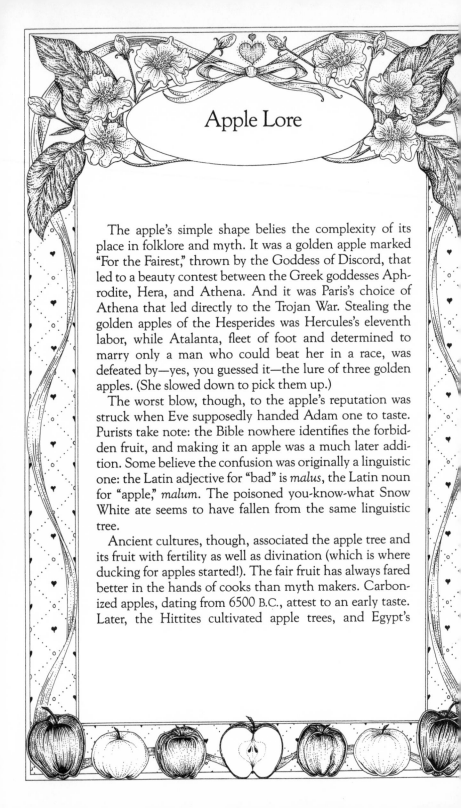

Apple Lore

The apple's simple shape belies the complexity of its place in folklore and myth. It was a golden apple marked "For the Fairest," thrown by the Goddess of Discord, that led to a beauty contest between the Greek goddesses Aphrodite, Hera, and Athena. And it was Paris's choice of Athena that led directly to the Trojan War. Stealing the golden apples of the Hesperides was Hercules's eleventh labor, while Atalanta, fleet of foot and determined to marry only a man who could beat her in a race, was defeated by—yes, you guessed it—the lure of three golden apples. (She slowed down to pick them up.)

The worst blow, though, to the apple's reputation was struck when Eve supposedly handed Adam one to taste. Purists take note: the Bible nowhere identifies the forbidden fruit, and making it an apple was a much later addition. Some believe the confusion was originally a linguistic one: the Latin adjective for "bad" is *malus*, the Latin noun for "apple," *malum*. The poisoned you-know-what Snow White ate seems to have fallen from the same linguistic tree.

Ancient cultures, though, associated the apple tree and its fruit with fertility as well as divination (which is where ducking for apples started!). The fair fruit has always fared better in the hands of cooks than myth makers. Carbonized apples, dating from 6500 B.C., attest to an early taste. Later, the Hittites cultivated apple trees, and Egypt's

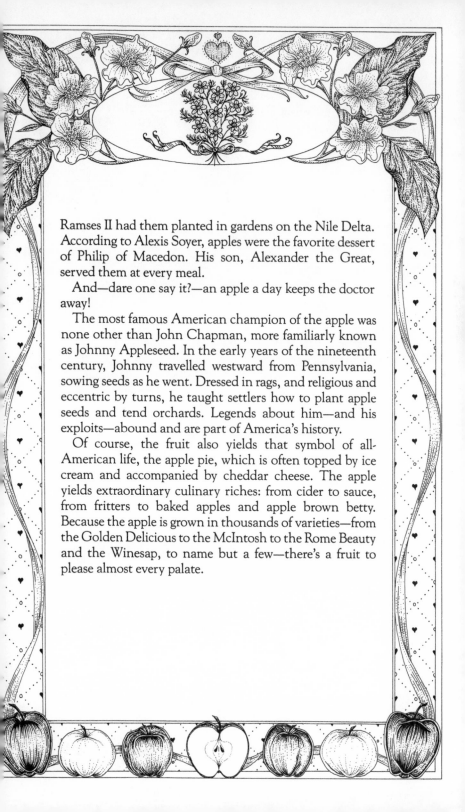

Ramses II had them planted in gardens on the Nile Delta. According to Alexis Soyer, apples were the favorite dessert of Philip of Macedon. His son, Alexander the Great, served them at every meal.

And—dare one say it?—an apple a day keeps the doctor away!

The most famous American champion of the apple was none other than John Chapman, more familiarly known as Johnny Appleseed. In the early years of the nineteenth century, Johnny travelled westward from Pennsylvania, sowing seeds as he went. Dressed in rags, and religious and eccentric by turns, he taught settlers how to plant apple seeds and tend orchards. Legends about him—and his exploits—abound and are part of America's history.

Of course, the fruit also yields that symbol of all-American life, the apple pie, which is often topped by ice cream and accompanied by cheddar cheese. The apple yields extraordinary culinary riches: from cider to sauce, from fritters to baked apples and apple brown betty. Because the apple is grown in thousands of varieties—from the Golden Delicious to the McIntosh to the Rome Beauty and the Winesap, to name but a few—there's a fruit to please almost every palate.

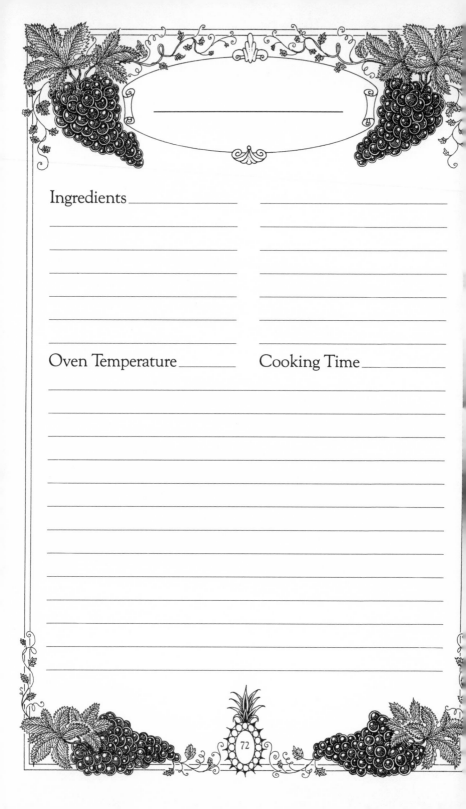

Ingredients

Oven Temperature_____ Cooking Time_____

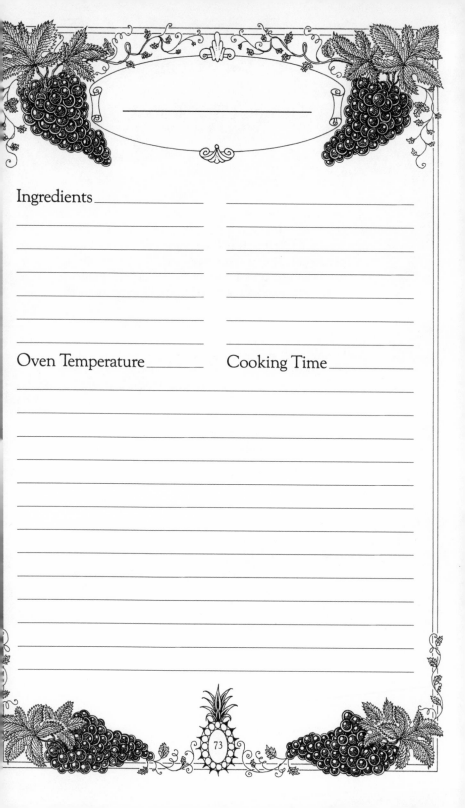

Ingredients

Oven Temperature_____   Cooking Time_____

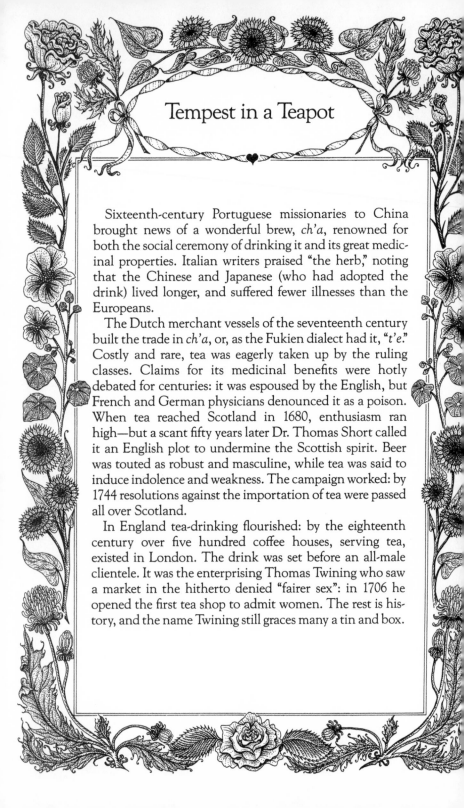

Tempest in a Teapot

Sixteenth-century Portuguese missionaries to China brought news of a wonderful brew, *ch'a*, renowned for both the social ceremony of drinking it and its great medicinal properties. Italian writers praised "the herb," noting that the Chinese and Japanese (who had adopted the drink) lived longer, and suffered fewer illnesses than the Europeans.

The Dutch merchant vessels of the seventeenth century built the trade in *ch'a*, or, as the Fukien dialect had it, "*t'e*." Costly and rare, tea was eagerly taken up by the ruling classes. Claims for its medicinal benefits were hotly debated for centuries: it was espoused by the English, but French and German physicians denounced it as a poison. When tea reached Scotland in 1680, enthusiasm ran high—but a scant fifty years later Dr. Thomas Short called it an English plot to undermine the Scottish spirit. Beer was touted as robust and masculine, while tea was said to induce indolence and weakness. The campaign worked: by 1744 resolutions against the importation of tea were passed all over Scotland.

In England tea-drinking flourished: by the eighteenth century over five hundred coffee houses, serving tea, existed in London. The drink was set before an all-male clientele. It was the enterprising Thomas Twining who saw a market in the hitherto denied "fairer sex": in 1706 he opened the first tea shop to admit women. The rest is history, and the name Twining still graces many a tin and box.

Ingredients_____ _____

_____ _____

_____ _____

_____ _____

_____ _____

_____ _____

_____ _____

Oven Temperature_____ Cooking Time_____

_____

_____

_____

_____

_____

_____

_____

_____

_____

_____

_____

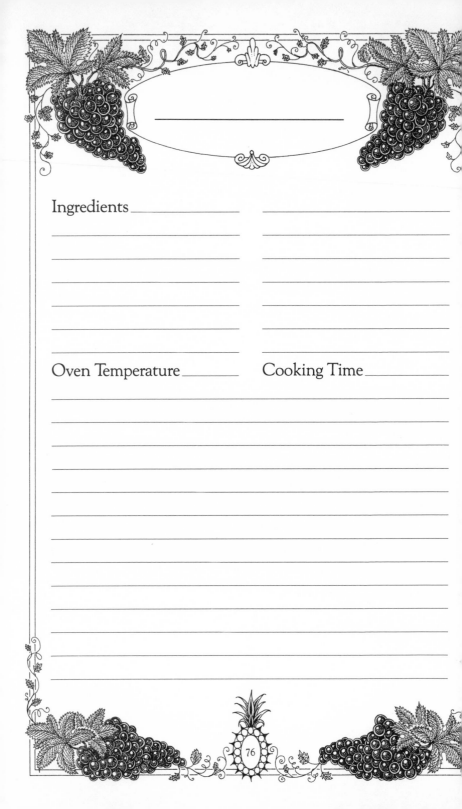

Ingredients _____

Oven Temperature _____

Cooking Time _____

Ingredients

_____ _____
_____ _____
_____ _____
_____ _____
_____ _____
_____ _____
_____ _____

Oven Temperature_____ Cooking Time_____

_____
_____
_____
_____
_____
_____
_____
_____
_____
_____
_____
_____
_____

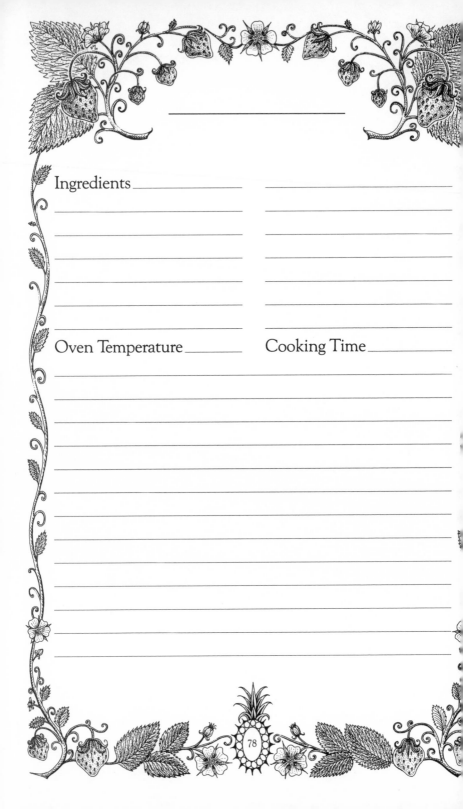

Ingredients

Oven Temperature_____   Cooking Time_____

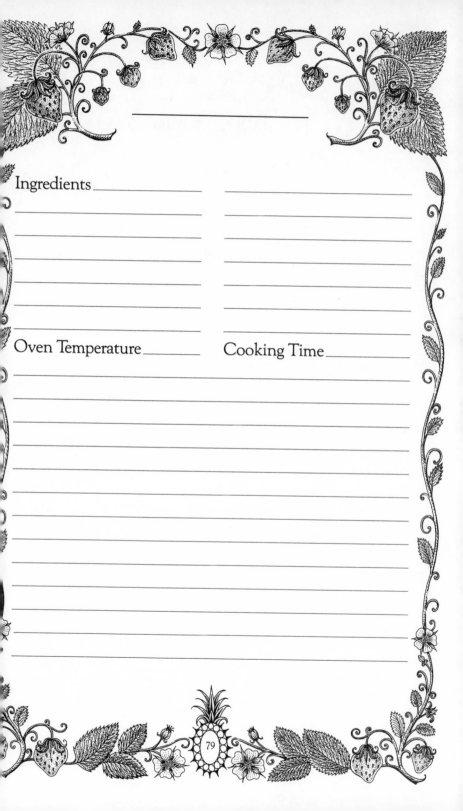

Ingredients_____

Oven Temperature_____   Cooking Time_____

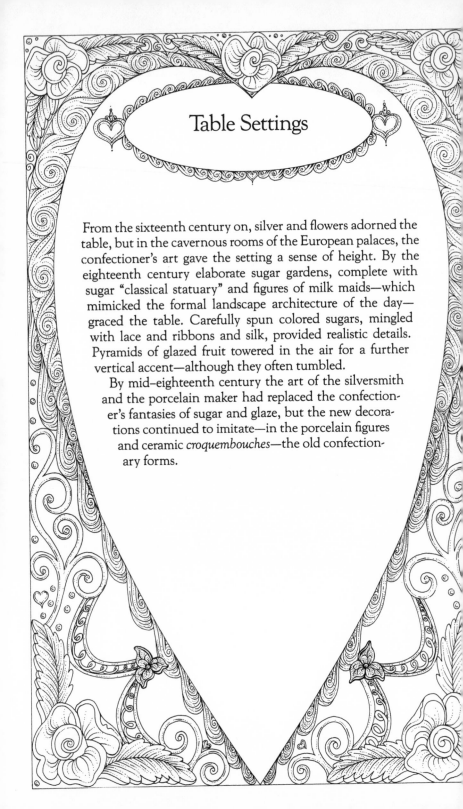

Table Settings

From the sixteenth century on, silver and flowers adorned the table, but in the cavernous rooms of the European palaces, the confectioner's art gave the setting a sense of height. By the eighteenth century elaborate sugar gardens, complete with sugar "classical statuary" and figures of milk maids—which mimicked the formal landscape architecture of the day—graced the table. Carefully spun colored sugars, mingled with lace and ribbons and silk, provided realistic details. Pyramids of glazed fruit towered in the air for a further vertical accent—although they often tumbled.

By mid-eighteenth century the art of the silversmith and the porcelain maker had replaced the confectioner's fantasies of sugar and glaze, but the new decorations continued to imitate—in the porcelain figures and ceramic *croquembouches*—the old confectionary forms.

Ingredients

Oven Temperature _____ Cooking Time _____

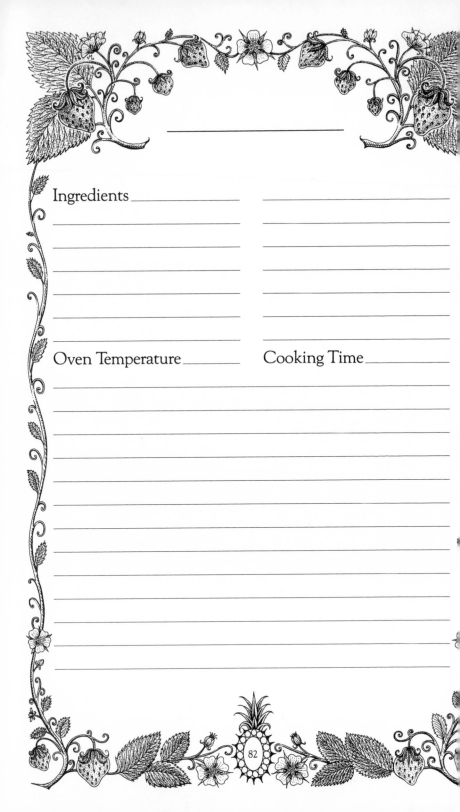

Ingredients _____ _____

_____ _____

_____ _____

_____ _____

_____ _____

_____ _____

_____ _____

Oven Temperature_____ Cooking Time_____

_____

_____

_____

_____

_____

_____

_____

_____

_____

_____

_____

_____

_____

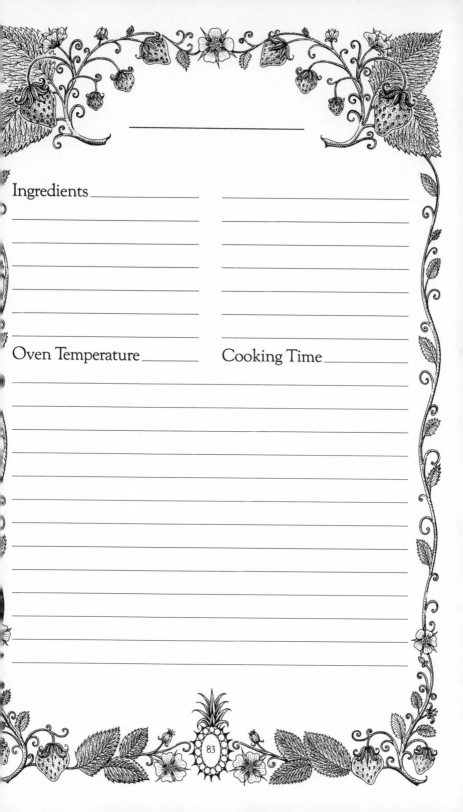

Ingredients_____ _____

_____ _____
_____ _____
_____ _____
_____ _____
_____ _____
_____ _____

Oven Temperature_____ Cooking Time_____

_____
_____
_____
_____
_____
_____
_____
_____
_____
_____
_____
_____
_____

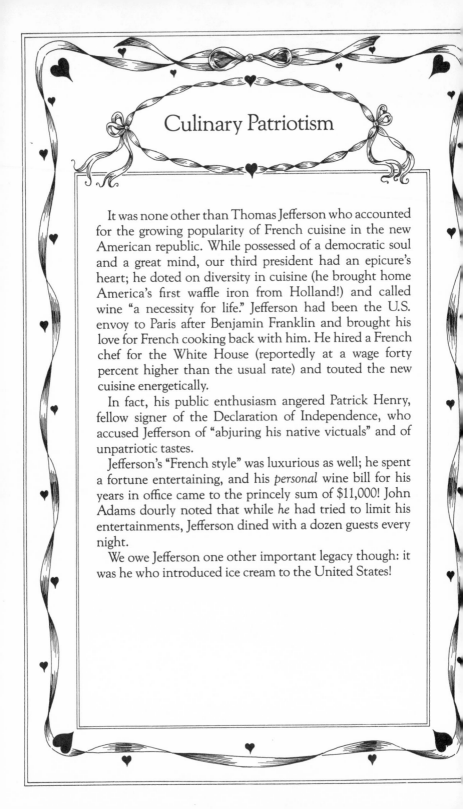

Culinary Patriotism

It was none other than Thomas Jefferson who accounted for the growing popularity of French cuisine in the new American republic. While possessed of a democratic soul and a great mind, our third president had an epicure's heart; he doted on diversity in cuisine (he brought home America's first waffle iron from Holland!) and called wine "a necessity for life." Jefferson had been the U.S. envoy to Paris after Benjamin Franklin and brought his love for French cooking back with him. He hired a French chef for the White House (reportedly at a wage forty percent higher than the usual rate) and touted the new cuisine energetically.

In fact, his public enthusiasm angered Patrick Henry, fellow signer of the Declaration of Independence, who accused Jefferson of "abjuring his native victuals" and of unpatriotic tastes.

Jefferson's "French style" was luxurious as well; he spent a fortune entertaining, and his *personal* wine bill for his years in office came to the princely sum of $11,000! John Adams dourly noted that while *he* had tried to limit his entertainments, Jefferson dined with a dozen guests every night.

We owe Jefferson one other important legacy though: it was he who introduced ice cream to the United States!

Special Occasions

Menu

Served on the occasion of _____

_____ on _____

Our guests were _____

_____

_____

Hors d'oeuvres: _____

_____

Main Course: _____

_____

Accompaniments: _____

_____

Dessert: _____

_____

Beverages: _____

_____

The table was set with _____ and decorated with

_____

_____

Menu

Served on the occasion of _____

_____ on _____

Our guests were _____

_____

_____

Hors d'oeuvres: _____

Main Course: _____

Accompaniments: _____

Dessert: _____

Beverages: _____

The table was set with _____ and decorated with

_____

_____

Menu

Served on the occasion of _____

_____ on _____

Our guests were _____

_____

_____

Hors d'oeuvres: _____

                          _____

Main Course: _____

                          _____

Accompaniments: _____

                          _____

Dessert: _____

                          _____

Beverages: _____

                          _____

The table was set with_____ and decorated with

_____

_____

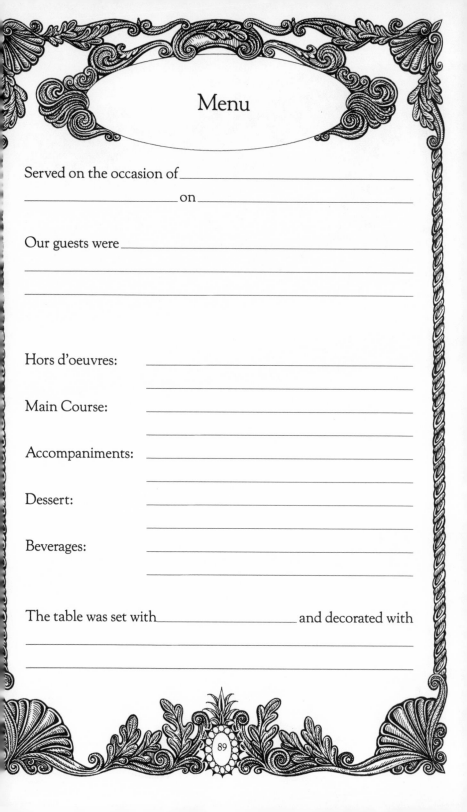

Menu

Served on the occasion of _____

_____ on _____

Our guests were _____

_____

_____

Hors d'oeuvres: _____

_____

Main Course: _____

_____

Accompaniments: _____

_____

Dessert: _____

_____

Beverages: _____

_____

The table was set with_____ and decorated with

_____

_____

Menu

Served on the occasion of_____

_____ on_____

Our guests were_____

_____

_____

Hors d'oeuvres: _____

                         _____

Main Course: _____

                         _____

Accompaniments: _____

                         _____

Dessert: _____

                         _____

Beverages: _____

                         _____

The table was set with_____ and decorated with

_____

_____

Menu

Served on the occasion of _____

_____ on _____

Our guests were _____

_____

_____

Hors d'oeuvres: _____

_____

Main Course: _____

_____

Accompaniments: _____

_____

Dessert: _____

_____

Beverages: _____

_____

The table was set with _____ and decorated with

_____

_____

Menu

Served on the occasion of _____

_____ on _____

Our guests were _____

_____

_____

Hors d'oeuvres: _____

_____

Main Course: _____

_____

Accompaniments: _____

_____

Dessert: _____

_____

Beverages: _____

_____

The table was set with _____ and decorated with

_____

_____

Menu

Served on the occasion of _____

_____ on _____

Our guests were _____

_____

_____

Hors d'oeuvres: _____

_____

Main Course: _____

_____

Accompaniments: _____

_____

Dessert: _____

_____

Beverages: _____

_____

The table was set with _____ and decorated with

_____

_____

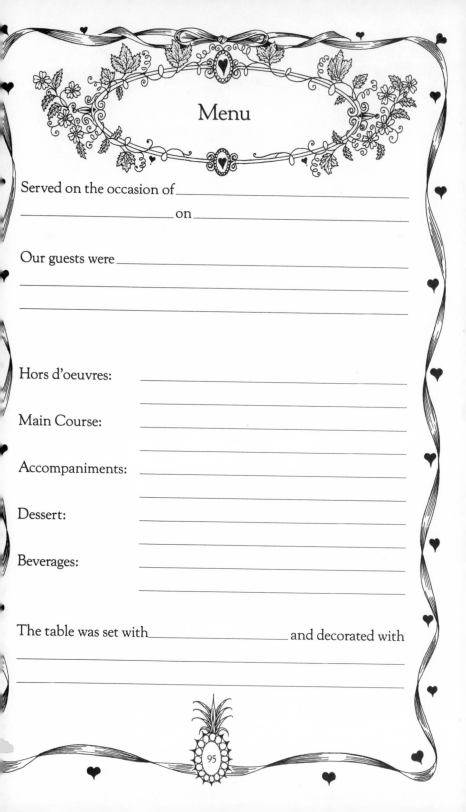

Menu

Served on the occasion of _____
_____ on _____

Our guests were _____
_____
_____

Hors d'oeuvres: _____

Main Course: _____

Accompaniments: _____

Dessert: _____

Beverages: _____

The table was set with _____ and decorated with
_____
_____

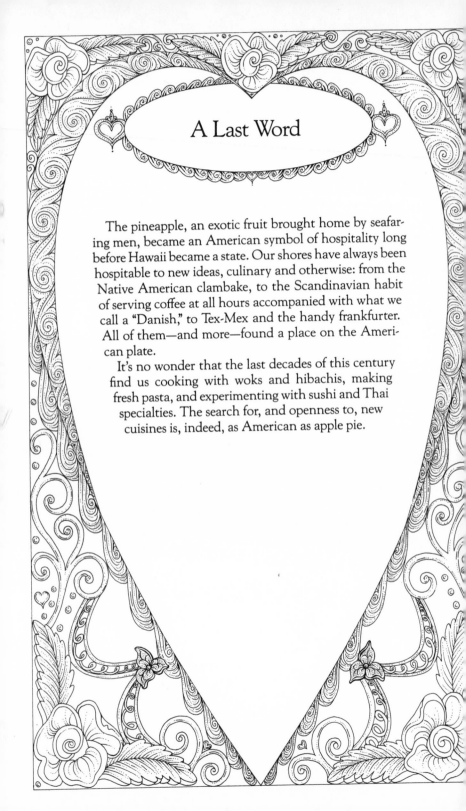

A Last Word

The pineapple, an exotic fruit brought home by seafaring men, became an American symbol of hospitality long before Hawaii became a state. Our shores have always been hospitable to new ideas, culinary and otherwise: from the Native American clambake, to the Scandinavian habit of serving coffee at all hours accompanied with what we call a "Danish," to Tex-Mex and the handy frankfurter. All of them—and more—found a place on the American plate.

It's no wonder that the last decades of this century find us cooking with woks and hibachis, making fresh pasta, and experimenting with sushi and Thai specialties. The search for, and openness to, new cuisines is, indeed, as American as apple pie.